D1536558

Claudia Ricci

The Church of Santa Felicita in Florence

Mandragora

© 2000 Mandragora. All rights reserved.

La Mandragora s.r.l.
piazza Duomo 9, 50122 Firenze
www.mandragora.it

Scientific Consultant: Francesca Fiorelli Malesci

English Translation: Alice Scott

Photography: Mandragora Archives, Antonio Quattrone,
Andrea Bazzechi, Marco Arduino

Printed in Italy

ISBN 88-85957-50-1

This book is printed on TCF (totally chlorine free) paper.

Presentation

Crossing over the Ponte Vecchio and heading towards the Pitti Palace, Florentines and tourists suddenly come upon the small square of Santa Felicita where the church of the same name and the Vasari Corridor meet in a unique and peculiar architectural complex.

It is difficult to forget the strong feeling of unity, harmony and beauty aroused by the sight of the interior of Santa Felicita from the window overlooking the Vasari Corridor. It is equally difficult, however, to imagine – with the exception of the Ponte Vecchio, the only bridge spanning the Arno at that time – just how different this area must have been between the 4th and 5th century AD. Here a disorderly suburb had grown outside the city walls: it was the crossroads to Rome, Siena, Arezzo and Pisa and the meeting point of caravans from all corners of the empire, guided by the changing vicissitudes of history.

It was against this backdrop that a group of Christians of Greek language and culture created the first nucleus of faith and cult, founding the early Christian Basilica and its cemetery. It is highly probable that the veneration of the early martyrs of the faith first began here. Thus a long history of construction and reconstruction exalting the Christian faith was started, constantly renewed with stimuli and impulses from art, painting and architecture – most notably in the second half of the 16th century, when Santa Felicita became the parish church of the ruling house and Vasari incorporated it in the grand-ducal quarters by means of the Corridor that connected the royal residence to the Uffizi.

The aim of this guidebook of the Church of Santa Felicita, published by Mandragora, is to be informative but serious and well-documented at the same time. Its purpose is to communicate with the public who visit the church but also to help them come in contact with the great Christian culture to which this church was witness. It is the tool which will help them read the history of a church where the encounter of oriental Christianity with the Church of Rome took place: a religious experience which in its turn would blend with the one developing on the other side of the city around the Church of San Lorenzo, brought forth by St. Ambrose's predication. It was the beginning of Florence's Christian journey.

Art and faith, order and harmony unite and enhance each other in turn to celebrate the beauty and joy of living. The publication of this guide gives us the opportunity to express one hope and desire: that the harmony of art and the light of faith may continue to inspire the third millennium as they have done for the last two thousand years.

Our sincere gratitude to all those who have contributed, with their work and competence, to the success of this publication.

don Mino Tagliaferri
parish priest of Santa Felicita

Introduction

In 1565 Giorgio Vasari, on the request of Cosimo de' Medici, soon to become the first grand-duke of Tuscany, built an overhead passageway from Palazzo Vecchio to the Pitti Palace. This long indoor gallery, later known as the Vasari Corridor, was destined for the private use of the ruling family. In this way they could move easily from their residence in the Oltrarno (the south bank of the Arno) to the government headquarters.

The Corridor gave new importance to an area which had played a vital role in Roman *Florentia*. In ancient times its central point, corresponding to the façade of Santa Felicita, gave access to the *coretto* ('little choir') of the church, a small private room from which the members of the grand-ducal family could attend the religious functions and then, by way of a stone staircase, reach the

Facing page: the Church of Santa Felicita in the square with the same name. Located near the Ponte Vecchio and the Pitti Palace, the church lies in the centre of one of the most suggestive itineraries in the historical centre of Florence. On the left one can see the Piazzetta de' Rossi which goes towards the Costa San Giorgio, one of the roads climbing up towards Fort Belvedere and leading to Viale dei Colli. Behind the building are many small lanes winding along the hillside, past unusual and picturesque places such as the small Arco della Mezzaluna ('Crescent Arch'). Left: the outside loggia of Santa Felicita, built at the same time as the Vasari Corridor. During the 18th-century reconstruction some of the sepulchral monuments inside the church were transferred here. On the left are the tombstone of Barduccio di Chierichino Barducci (ca. 1416) in late Gothic style and the sepulchral monument of Arcangiola Paladini *by Agostino Bugiardini (Florence ca.1590-1623), completed by his pupil Antonio Novelli (Castelfranco di Sopra, Arezzo 1600-Florence 1662); on either side of the bust are allegories of music and painting, arts in which Arcangiola Paladini, the favourite artist of Grand-Duchess Mary Magdalen of Austria, distinguished herself.*

main chapel to receive the sacraments. Today a large window offers the visitor walking through the Corridor from the Uffizi Gallery one of the most imposing views of the interior of the church.

It is thus possible to reach the square of Santa Felicita through the Vasari Corridor, after having crossed the Ponte Vecchio and turned into Via Guicciardini. Here the Corridor juts out from the buildings around it and, after a bend, leans against the façade of the church. The large overhanging *loggia* partly conceals with its sloping roof the big central window and the three ancient coats of arms of the Guicciardini family. This family had always been the patrons of the church and their property was situated in this parish.

Today the church has a completely different look from its ancient origins. Only the exterior reveals signs of its medieval past: the interior was entirely reconstructed by Ferdinando Ruggieri in the years 1736 to 1739, and very few of the works that decorated the chapels and the altars before this reconstruction have survived. In the external *loggia* one can see the 15th-century tombstone of Barduccio di Chierichino Barducci, the monument to Cardinal Luigi de' Rossi (a 16th-century work by Giovan Battista Del Tasso) and the monument to Arcangiola Paladini, the favourite painter and musician of Mary Magdalen of Austria (17th century), all of which were moved here during the reconstruction. Most of the gilded altarpieces which, according to the documents, were numer-

The marble sepulchre of Cardinal Luigi de' Rossi *(first half of the 16th century), on the right wall of the loggia of Santa Felicita. Traditionally attributed to Raffaello da Montelupo, this monument has only recently been recognized as the work of architect and sculptor Giovan Battista del Tasso. On either side of the base, elaborately sculpted, is the coat of arms of the de' Rossi family. The Cardinal was also portrayed by Raphael – together with Pope Leo X and Cardinal Giulio de' Medici (the future Pope Clement VII) – in a famous painting now in the Uffizi.*

The interior of the Church of Santa Felicita was entirely reconstructed between 1736 and 1739 by the Florentine architect and engraver Ferdinando Ruggieri (Florence 1691-1741). A vaulted ceiling with double arches and large windows in 'pietra serena' substituted the original wooden trusses, while a sense of harmony was obtained in the nave by the introduction of a series of identical chapels.
Below: the famous Carta della Catena *(see p. 14) shows the city around 1470. In this detail one can see on the left the Romanesque façade of Santa Felicita, with a portal above which there is a lunette-shaped 'architrave', surmounted by a single central window (Florence, "Firenze com'era" Museum).*

ous, were either lost or relocated elsewhere. All this was done in the name of modernity and a change of taste: a practice which would lead to the impoverishment of this and many other ancient churches.

As far as the transformation of the interior is concerned, Ruggieri replaced the original wooden trusses of the roof with the double-vaulted ceiling in *pietra serena* and the elegant large windows that terminate in luminous groins whose visual impact is enhanced by daylight. The nave (more or less the same length as that of the medieval structure, and only a little wider) is graced with mirroring chapels at equal intervals which give movement to the simple dichromatic white and grey of the walls and replaced the stratifications that resulted from the expansion of the building from the 11th to the beginning of the 18th century. Regarding the works which were carried out on the ancient interior, Giuseppe Richa, the 18th-century au-

thor to whom we owe a fundamental text on Florentine churches, wrote with regret: "it was necessary to destroy, not only the nave, by cutting the large and small altars, but also the fine marbles and monuments placed against the walls" (G. Richa, IX, 1761, p. 313), efficiently describing a space full of fixed and mobile structures, in contrast with the present, rather sparse, arrangement.

The protruding structure of the two small chapels in front of the transept is particularly well conceived. With their pairs of columns, they present the main chapel in clear perspective. The two balconies, whose balustrades are identical to that of the grand-ducal *coretto* on the internal façade, represent, with their upper part framed by tablet scrolls, the most evident concession to late Baroque style.

View of the interior of the church from the high altar. On the façade wall, the small balcony of the 'coretto' from which the grand-dukes attended the religious ceremonies.

1. History: 4th-20th century

The origins

The present-day characteristics of the church and of the adjacent convent appear to be fairly recent; in actual fact this complex has very ancient origins, witnessed by the existence of documents prior to the year one thousand and to the presence of early Christian burial remains. From the ruins it can be deduced that the convent had reached huge proportions, at least from the middle of the 14th century. It is therefore necessary to reconstruct as accurately as possible how the church actually looked before its last reconstruction which dates back to the 18th century.

The devotion of the church to St. Felicita also has an early origin. The original name of the basilica – first attested in a document dated 972 – seems to have been taken from the Roman Felicita who, together with her seven children, was martyr under Emperor Antoninus Pius (2nd century AD). As there were also seven Maccabees brothers in the Bible, popular tradition immediately identified the Saint as their mother, whose martyrdom (2nd century BC) is mentioned in the Old Testament. It is probable that the adjacent Christian cemetery was dedicated to the Maccabees, whose cult was very much alive in the early centuries of Christianity.

Under Hadrian (117-138 AD) Florence had flourished thanks to its strategic position along important commercial routes. On the left bank of the Arno – where the ancient and only bridge of the times crossed the river, more or less where we now have the Ponte Vecchio – two important routes departed: the Cassia, starting from the present Via Guicciardini and headed for Rome, and the Pisana, the first stretch of which coincides with Borgo San Jacopo.

At that time an Eastern Greek-speaking colony settled in the area, and it is believed that they are responsible for bringing Christianity to the city. The first basilica was built between the 4th and 5th century in this very same area. The Greek and Latin tombstones put in the wall of the rectory corridor (accessible from the entrance on the right of the façade) from 1749 on date back to this period.

Below: one of the memorial stones walled up in the rectory corridor in the 18th century, testifying to the ancient origins of Santa Felicita.
The finds coming from the remnants of the early Christian cemetery – discovered during the works undertaken by Ruggieri and, later, while laying the foundation of a pillar of the Vasari Corridor (1749) – were studied by well-known Florentine scholars such as Anton Francesco Gori, Domenico Maria Manni and Giovanni Lami.

The large ruins of the building, found under the present church, began to emerge during the excavation of 1933. Mined in 1944 by the retreating German troops, after the war the area was subject to further research, which in 1948 revealed the existence of an early Christian basilica, 38 metres long and 26 metres wide, with a nave and two aisles, and a semicircular apse. Built to the west of the present church, but with the same orientation, the basilica had a much wider façade. Its foundation was about two and a half metres below the present floor level, and the floor was made up of tomb covers upon which lapidary inscriptions were laid together with their decorative elements.

The Middle Ages

Following the decline of the early Christian temple, the survival of the place of cult was entrusted to a fairly humble building. This structure had already deteriorated considerably in 1059 when Pope Nicholas II decided to reconstruct and reconsecrate the church together with its adjacent Benedictine convent.

In the 11th century AD, in a period of significant economic and demographic growth, Florence – as a result of its pre-eminent role in the struggles between the Papacy and the Empire – became a centre of intensive con-

The Benedictine convent, reconsecrated in 1059 by Pope Nicholas II, was frescoed at the end of the 14th century by Niccolò di Pietro Gerini († ca. 1414). The fine decoration by the Florentine painter is still visible in the chapter-house. The two fragments of frescoes depicting Prophets *(above) were detached from the vaults of the chapter-house in the 19th century and are now in the sacristy. Right:* The Nativity, *a work attributed to the school of Gerini. The original location of the fresco, now in the 'scarsella' of the sacristy, is unknown. There is no doubt, however, that it was not part of the chapter-house cycle, since techniques for the detachment of frescoes did not exist at the time the decoration was concluded (1665).*

struction of new buildings, as well as the restructuring of ancient ones. A particular interest in the city was shown by its bishop Gerardo who, upon becoming Pope Nicholas II, dedicated his attention not only to Santa Felicita but also to San Lorenzo and to Santi Michele ed Eusebio.

The historical and topographic elements which gave rise to the medieval church and convent were identical to those at the origin of the early Christian basilica. Each church served as a reference point for the civic and daily life of the medieval city. The convent played an even more significant role in gathering the citizens of Oltrarno, because in the 11th century the district was still situated outside the city walls and was linked to the rest of the city by a single bridge. During the same period the *borgo* became the meeting point of the inhabitants of the *contado*, inhabitants coming mainly from the surrounding rural areas, who had settled in the city. The property and the real estate policy of the convent played a decisive role in the demographic expansion and the building development of the area. Besides being owners of building sites, the religious centres drew advantages from the growth of the population: hence, they were the focal points of new settlements.

Above: a detail of The Martyrdom of St. Catherine of Alexandria, *a work attributed to a contemporary of Gerini. According to sources the fresco was in the first chapel on the left of the high altar, which was demolished by Ferdinando Ruggieri during the 18th-century reconstruction. Detached from the walls during restoration work to the church after the flood of 1966, the fresco is now housed in the corridor next to the cloister.*
Left: fragment of a painting of the Gerini school, on the same level as The Nativity *on the wall opposite the 'scarsella' of the sacristy. The fresco, which has been recomposed by a complex work of restoration, depicts* The Annunciation.

Above: the 14th-century cloister. The archways – walled up in the 18th century – are supported by columns ending in 'water-leaf' capitals: such a style suggests for the structure a date around the year 1340. Below: a detail of the wall facing the entrance.

It is in this economic and social context that we should imagine the new Church of Santa Felicita, which we shall define, for our convenience, 'Romanesque'. The ruins of the construction, mostly found during the excavations of 1933 and 1948, are limited to the apse (which, according to the architectural practice of the period, had been inserted into that of the 5th-century basilica), and to four columns with porphyry capitals, now reduced to three. These columns are now part of the modern structures of the rectory and are visible on the right side of the building.

Our historical knowledge of the building is therefore based on inadequate information, a fact which has led to mistaken interpretations and reconstructions in the past. Iconographic complement to the existing documentation concerning the period from the 12th to the 14th century are the external views of the church found in the maps of the Codex Vaticanus 5699 and the so-called *Carta della Catena* (see p. 9), both datable to the seventies of the 15th century. Although the two views are completely different in composition and layout, they show us a church of small dimensions, on the slopes of the hill of San Giorgio, with its belfry on the left. Both in the longitudinal view of the Vaticanus (which also shows the little side door looking onto the Piazzetta de' Rossi) and in the frontal view of the *Carta*, the church appears as a typical Romanesque structure with a sloping roof and a linear façade, on which there is a semicircular architraved portal, surmounted by a central circular window.

The 14th century

It is this building, and not the hypothetical Gothic construction believed to have been built towards the middle of the 14th century, that was reconstructed in the 18th century. It should be remembered, however, that it had already been transformed by several works of maintenance and adornment, undertaken from the second half of the 14th century, when the patrons carried out major works in the interior of the church. During this period the interest of private citizens, especially of the families living in the same square or in the nearby roads of the district, expressed itself through the building of altars and chapels in Santa Felicita. All this took place in a more general situation in which the wealthy classes were trying to find a more concrete token of their faith and prestige in the adornment of the family chapel with decorations and church furnishings. Offerings through a memorial tomb or a work of art by those who had escaped the dangers of the Plague in 1348 also played an important role. It is no coincidence that in the years immediately following the terrible epidemic, the number of wills in favour of monasteries, con-

Below: a 14th-century polyptych attributed to Taddeo Gaddi († before 1366), depicting a Madonna with Child and Saints (ca. 1355). In the cusps are represented various Prophets and, beneath the Virgin, four angels. The names of the Saints are indicated on the inscriptions (from the left: Jacob, John the Baptist, Luke and Philip). On the lower level are alternated the coats of arms of the Guicciardini and Guidetti families.

Above: a work by Neri di Bicci († ca. 1476), St. Felicita and Children. The painting, executed between 1463 and 1464 for the Nerli Chapel, was put in the sacristy after a long and complex restoration. Below the Saint is a small Crucifixion. The 'predella' is decorated with scenes of The Martyrdom of the Sons of St. Felicita; as can be seen on the right in the detail on the facing page, the torturers' faces have been completely obliterated.

vents and other religious communities increased substantially, and that alongside the foundation of chapels and the desire for sumptuous burials – abundantly testified in our church as well as in others – new religious centres were founded in many areas throughout the city.

The nave of the 14th-century church was decorated with altars and chapels which were nothing more than large tabernacles placed on steps. On the sides of the main chapel were the Barducci Chapel of St. Catherine and the Mannelli Chapel of St. John the Evangelist; along the left wall, that of the Canigiani family and the altars of the Rossi and Guicciardini families. One of these altars perhaps housed the polyptych with the *Madonna and Saints* by Taddeo Gaddi, now in the sacristy. On the right were the altars of St. Gregory and St. Bartholomew as well as the Pitti Chapel dedicated to St. Sebastian.

However, the most important commission in the 14th century was not made by a private citizen but by the abbess Lorenza de' Mozzi who in 1395 commissioned the painting for the high altar. The polyptych with *The Coronation of the Virgin and Saints* – signed by Niccolò Gerini, Spinello Aretino and Lorenzo di Niccolò in 1399 – was transferred to the Accademia after the ecclesiastic suppressions of 1810. In the same year the church was enriched – once again as the result of a monastic commission – by the stained-glass window that gave light to the main chapel and by the frescoes inside the chapel itself, begun by Neri d'Antonio and completed upon his death by an unknown artist. Nothing has survived of these works as a result of the numerous restorations performed in the apse in subsequent years.

The important works in the Benedictine convent date back to the end of the 14th century. This convent, which no longer exists today, had been consecrated in 1059 by Pope Nicholas II together with the medieval church: Niccolò di Pietro Gerini painted the frescoes in the chapter-house, the only part which still preserves its architectural and decorative identity. Gerini worked – perhaps at a later period – on the walls of the church and the adjacent convent as well. Several paintings of which only fragments have survived are attributed to him and to his school. This is particularly the case with two frescoes – already detached in the 19th century – depicting *The Annunciation* and *The Nativity* (now in the sacristy), and *The Martyrdom of St. Catherine*, placed in the side corridor of the cloister after restoration.

The 15th and 16th centuries

A moment of great cultural and artistic renewal, the 15th century is also a witness of numerous important architectural and decorative interventions inside Santa Felicita. Many altars and chapels were built, and numerous paint-

Among the works housed today in the sacristy of Santa Felicita is a lunette by Bicci di Lorenzo (Florence 1373-1452) representing The Mystical Marriage of St. Catherine. *The work, which was probably part of the furnishings of the chapter-house, dates back to 1442.*

ings appeared above the altars. The church underwent a rigorous work of construction, leaving behind the decorative fragmentation which had been its most characteristic trait throughout the 14th century.

Over the centuries many of the paintings completed during these years have been put away – for reasons of cult and especially of taste – in the convent or in the sacristy. *The Three Archangels and Tobiolo* by Domenico di Michelino and the painting executed by Bicci di Lorenzo for the Chapel of San Frediano, built between 1436 and 1437 after the death of Donato, son of Bartolomeo Barbadori, are no longer in the church: the former is now at the Accademia, while the latter has been lost. The only surviving trace of this chapel is an elegant mosaic portrait of Alessandro Barbadori (now kept in a room in the parish buildings), executed in Rome in 1649 by Marcello Provenzale. However, the finding of the complete documentation concerning these works has enabled a step-by-step study of its construction and of the expenses sustained for the decorations.

A typical example of the wealth of the patrons is the Barbadori Chapel by Brunelleschi, built in this period. Another important undertaking of those years was the sacristy: its design clearly influenced by Brunelleschi's ideas, it was financed by a legacy of Giovanni Canigiani (1474).

The first part of the 16th century thus ended with Santa Felicita as the centre of fundamental artistic experiences within the city. It also marked the end of total autonomy: from 1565 – the year of the construction of the Corridor by Vasari – its vicissitudes became closely linked not only to private patrons but also to the influence of the grandduchy. Santa Felicita, although one of the three Florentine churches in which jubilee years were celebrated, had never enjoyed any special public attention. This was also due to its decentralized position, far from the civic and administrative life of the city: it now became the focal centre of the ceremonies and everyday religious events of the rulers.

The first move with which the Medici established this bond – destined to grow stronger, especially with the nuns of the adjacent convent – consisted in the construction of that very same corridor which, besides offering an excellent view of the interior, was also later enlarged with a room built over the façade chapels, to enable the grand-dukes to attend the religious ceremonies without mingling with the people. The building of this room – known as the *coretto*

Left: the Barbadori Chapel – dedicated to the Virgin of the Annunciation and, from 1525 on, to the Pietà – was designed by Filippo Brunelleschi (Florence 1377-1446) between the second and third decade of the 15th century. The chapel underwent numerous interventions in the course of the centuries. In 1936 a restoration performed by Raffaello Niccoli brought to light its original structure. The square-planned chapel is closed on two sides by iron grating, while the arch is supported by Ionic half-columns. The domed ceiling, originally hemispherical, leans on four pendentives decorated by 'tondi' depicting the four Evangelists; the floor, only partially recovered by the restoration, was covered with white 'maiolica' tiles with blue 'ramages'.

since the end of the 17th century – probably dates back to the early years of the grand-duchy of Ferdinando I (1587-1609) and is connected to the habit, prevalent between the 17th and 18th century, of creating, independently from the private chapels inside the palaces, a convenient listening point in the churches closest to the residential quarters. Examples that still exist of this custom are the entrance to Santo Spirito from the Frescobaldi Palace, to Santi Apostoli from the Chapel of the Rosselli del Turco and to Santo Stefano al Ponte from the Bartolommei Palace.

The traditional participation of the ruling family in the religious ceremonies in the church, inaugurated by Ferdinando I and always observed by his successors (documents and chronicles give us ample information on Ferdinando II, Cosimo III and Pietro Leopoldo of Lorraine), can be explained by the desire to "represent" the religiousness of the grand-duke on a sort of ideal stage. It was this very desire of

the Medici to present themselves as a 'Catholic family' in the years following the Council of Trent, that induced Ferdinando I to promote this public expression of the religious life of the Prince, which had found another scenario in the Basilica of San Lorenzo. First Cosimo, who had obtained the title of grand-duke through the intervention of the Pope, then his successors, wanted to show – not only in their official policies, but also in their everyday life – Counter-reformation attitudes and a religious zeal which would leave its mark in the memories of their contemporaries.

Not even the construction, at a much later date, of the chapel inside the Pitti Palace – commissioned by Pietro Leopoldo and consecrated in 1766 – did bring any significant change in the religious habits of the rulers. The grand-dukes will always be present here in Santa Felicita: indeed, they will never abstain from this public display of piety just around the corner from their residence.

The 17th century

After the radical changes of the 16th century, the 17th witnessed only slight modifications, dictated by a new taste in architecture and decoration. The most important intervention was carried out by Ludovico Cigoli, who designed the new main chapel which had come under the patronage of the Guicciardini family since 1606. Other works – the Badii-Cioli altar in the left transept and the reliquary monument of St. Carlo Borromeo, placed in Brunelleschi's chapel and whose authors are unknown – are interesting only as examples of the Florentine taste for polychrome marble.

The works of the family chapel were supervised mostly by Piero Guicciardini. He had left for Rome in 1611 after being appointed ambassador, and reached an agreement with Cigoli, who had also been invited to Rome by Pope Clement VIII. However the work would undergo great difficulties due to protests and controversies resulting mainly from the artist's absence from the building site: owing to other commissions Cigoli was detained at the Vatican and returned to Florence only for very limited periods.

In Rome Piero commissioned several followers of Caravaggio with paintings destined to decorate the walls of the apse (the vault had been painted between 1617 and 1619 by Michelangelo Cinganelli). Detailed information on these works can be obtained from "The Registry of Commissions", in which the orders of payment made by Piero

Facing page, below, left: located in the left transept, The Holy Trinity, a 16th-century painting by Carlo Portelli. In the second decade of the 17th century Piero Guicciardini, ambassador to Rome, commissioned several works for the main chapel of Santa Felicita, some of which are no longer in the church: The Crucifixion by the Florentine artist Lorenzo Carletti (above, a detail) is now on the left wall of the chapel in the place of a painting with identical subject by Spadarino, while on the opposite wall – where there should have been a painting by Cecco del Caravaggio – is now The Resurrection of Christ by Antonio Tempesta (facing page, below, right). Above: St. Louis King of France Inviting the Poor to the Banquet by Simone Pignoni (detail). Executed in 1682, the painting is placed above the altar of St. Louis (left wall).

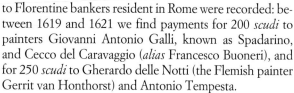

to Florentine bankers resident in Rome were recorded: between 1619 and 1621 we find payments for 200 *scudi* to painters Giovanni Antonio Galli, known as Spadarino, and Cecco del Caravaggio (*alias* Francesco Buoneri), and for 250 *scudi* to Gherardo delle Notti (the Flemish painter Gerrit van Honthorst) and Antonio Tempesta.

Only very few of the works mentioned among these commissions – and as such destined to Florence – are today in their place. *The Resurrection of Christ* by Cecco del Caravaggio never entered Santa Felicita; perhaps the patron did not approve of it. In its place was put a painting with an identical subject by Antonio Tempesta, still in the church. Among these orders there is also a *Crucifixion* mentioned as a work by Spadarino, but the painting we see today is by the Florentine painter Lorenzo Carletti: already mentioned in the 18th century, the work has recently been restored, but the restoration did not bring to light an underlying work by the Roman painter. However, it is possible that Carletti had to work on a highly deteriorated canvas, so that the pre-existing painting became completely unrecognizable.

The 18th century

In the 18th century the works executed in the preceding century – as well as older structures such as the Barbadori-Capponi and Canigiani chapels – found a worthy place in the new building designed by Ferdinando Ruggieri.

The nuns had already decided to reconstruct the church almost completely several years before: there are traces of this decision in the documents of the second decade of the century. During these years – required to deal with the various economic and organizational problems – they chose to appoint Ruggieri as official architect for the reconstruction. He was the most famous local artist of the time, as well as the most faithful to the canons of the late 16th-century architecture which was so fashionable in those years. Later a request was made to obtain the protection of the grandduke, but documents clearly show that this was just a formality, as the request was made after everything had already been decided. Despite the existence of the corridor with its *coretto* and the assiduous participation of the ruling family in the religious functions, the Medici never exerted any unpleasant interference on the convent, which always continued to be independent and sovereign. Although the grandducal "presence" in the church is attested by monuments

and tombstones such as those in the chapels underneath the choirs, numerous documents show that, except for the generosity of the parishioners, the works – from the minor interventions to the thorough reconstruction started in 1736 – were exclusively paid for by the Benedictine nuns.

The 19th century

After the significant reconstruction of the 18th century the prestige and importance of the convent began to decline. The first ecclesiastic suppression under Pietro Leopoldo (1785) became a peremptory order in 1787, but the nuns continued to live in the convent. In 1810, following the annexation of Tuscany to France, all the monasteries and convents were definitively suppressed and the property of the church sold. The history of the convent came to an end and the works in Santa Felicita were also suspended, except for small interventions undertaken by private citizens.

The construction of the new building, which one century before had aroused the admiration of the contemporaries, therefore coincided with the beginning of its decline. The Benedictine convent, fulcrum of activity, work and endeavours, gradually lost its importance both because of the reduced number of nuns and the political and religious events that struck Florence and Tuscany with the coming of the Lorraine. No longer sustained by the convent, from which it had originated, the church lost its vital role as a focal centre of attraction and aggregation which, century after century, had contributed to its emergence as an important parish under the grand-duchy.

Once again a parish church and an active religious and cultural centre within the city, Santa Felicita has now opened its almost unknown treasures to Florentines and foreign visitors who stop at the church on their way to the Pitti Palace, or who suddenly catch an unexpected glimpse of its interior from the Vasari Corridor.

Right: The Adoration of the Child *by Nicola Cianfanelli (Moscow 1793-Florence 1848). The painting, executed between 1828 and 1838 for the altar of the Pitti family, is located in the right transept of the church. Facing page: another (and finer) example of a 19th-century intervention on the interior of the church,* The Martyrdom of the Seven Maccabees Brothers *by Antonio Ciseri (Ronco, Chieti 1821-Florence 1891). Begun in 1853, the painting was placed above the third altar of the right wall.*

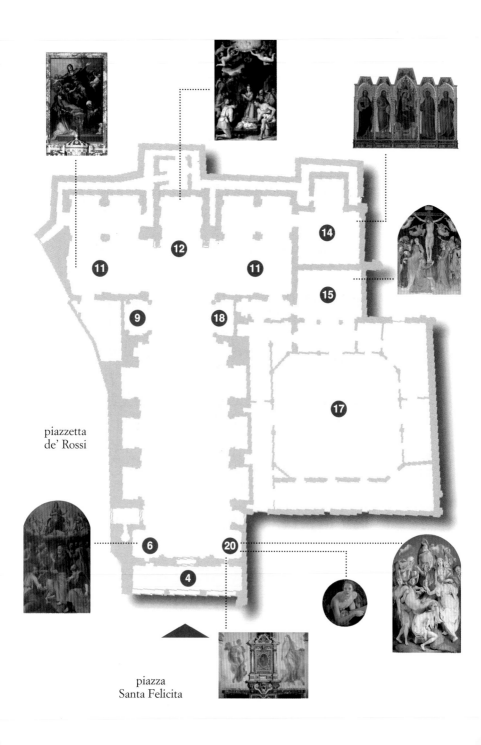

piazzetta
de' Rossi

piazza
Santa Felicita

1. 14th-century buttress
2. window of the Gothic church
3. Guicciardini coats of arms
4. Vasari Corridor and *loggia*
5. grand-ducal *coretto*
6. Canigiani Chapel
7. 14th-century corbels
8. passageway through the attic
9. organ platform
10. stairway to the platform
11. transept
12. main chapel
13. 14th-century frescoes
14. sacristy
15. chapter-house
16. Gothic column
17. cloister
18. choir of the nuns
19. Gothic wall
20. Barbadori-Capponi Chapel
21. 18th-century stairway

Santa Felicita:
plan and axonometric projection

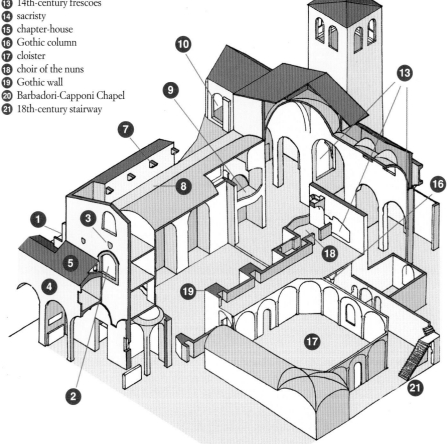

(from a drawing by Paolo Degl'Innocenti)

2. Itinerary

The interior. The numerous changes made over the centuries thwart the interpretation of the Romanesque façade, while the interior, although it includes two 15th- and 16th-century chapels and the Baroque chancel, is marked by the harmonious style and balanced sobriety typical of Florentine architecture in the first decades of the 18th century.

Between 1736 and 1739 Ferdinando Ruggieri designed an interior characterized by architectural elements distinctively rooted in 16th-century style, and still perfectly suited to the main chapel by Cigoli. Furthermore, to better har-

Facing page: a view of the nave and the apse of Santa Felicita. In the centre, the high altar which in 1840 replaced the 17th-century altar by Gherardo Silvani. Left: a view of the left wall. The Corinthian columns in 'pietra serena' enclose three chapels on either side of the nave.

monize the late 16th-century structure with the new 18th-century elements, the architect modified the final part of the front of the chapel: a split tympanum with the elegant Guicciardini coat of arms in the centre was placed above the original *architrave* by Cigoli. Elements drawn on Cigoli's style also include the denticulate moulding along the protruding *cornice* beneath the windows – already used by Ruggieri in the trabeation of the façade of San Filippo Neri – and the fluted pilaster strips which mark the succession of the chapels on the sides of the nave. To find examples which have some structural similarity to this interior, we have to go back to late 16th-century Florentine architecture, such as that of San Giovannino by Ammannati. Indeed there is nothing in common between the choices made by Ruggieri and those of the preceding generation of architects working in the 17th century in several churches of the city: Gherardo Silvani in San Gaetano, Antonio Cerutti and Antonio Ferri in San Frediano al Cestello.

The Canigiani Chapel ('dell'Assunta'). In 1589, as a result of the works for the *coretto* (erected, as we have mentioned, above the façade chapels), Giovanni di Antonio Canigiani decided to renew the Chapel of the Assunta ('Our Lady of the Assumption'), which had been under the patronage of the family since 1365. The aim of Bernardino Poccetti, who was commissioned with this intervention, was to create a companion to the facing Barbadori-Capponi Chapel, which

had just been decorated by Pontormo. And indeed both its structure and its decoration are closely linked to the earlier work by Brunelleschi. The artist conceived, in one of his first important frescoes, the *cupola* which probably depicted *The Holy Trinity* and four *tondi* with *Saints* by the name of John in honour of the patron. Like Pontormo's *cupola*, this work was destroyed between 1765 and 1767. It was later frescoed by Tommaso Gherardini, whose work is still visible. On the façade wall Poccetti painted a scene with *The Miracle of Our Lady of the Snow* (1589-90). *The Assumption of the Virgin*, an altarpiece by Andrea di Mariotto del Minga, completed the renewed chapel.

Facing page: The Assumption of the Virgin and Saints *by Andrea di Mariotto del Minga (? after 1540-Florence 1596). For many years the altarpiece had been attributed to Poccetti, but the finding of the documents concerning the payments has revealed the pupil of Giorgio Vasari as the true author of the work. It was painted for the Canigiani Chapel between 1589 and 1591. Below: on the façade wall of the same chapel,* The Miracle of Our Lady of the Snow on the Esquilino *(1589-1590) by Bernardino Poccetti. The fresco depicts the patrician Giovanni offering Pope Liberius the plan of the Roman Basilica of Santa Maria Maggiore to celebrate the miraculous summer snowfall of the year 352. Poccetti also painted four Saints by the name of John in the four 'tondi' in the pendentives of the vault in honour of the patron: John the Evangelist, John the Baptist (whose face recalls that of St. Matthew in the Barbadori Chapel), Giovanni Gualberto and John the Martyr.*

The left wall. On the first altar is *The Martyrdom of St. Sebastian* by Fabrizio Boschi, a work executed in 1617 upon the commission of the Canigiani family for the Chapel of St. Bartholomew the Apostle and St. Sebastian; on the second, *Tobias Visiting his Father* by Ignazio Hugford. The painting was commissioned in the 18th century to replace the aforementioned painting by Domenico di Michelino, now preserved in the Accademia. A follower of Anton Domenico Gabbiani, Hugford was a painter, restorer and art collector. Lastly, on the third altar is *St. Louis, King of France Inviting the Poor to the Banquet* (1682), one of the few works by Simone Pignoni with a public destination (see p. 21). Generally speaking, these works of art show us the high quality of Florentine painting between the 17th and the 18th century.

Facing page: The Martyrdom of St. Sebastian *by Fabrizio Boschi (Florence 1570-1642). The painting, executed for a chapel which no longer exists, was placed above the first altar of the left wall after the 18th-century reconstruction. Below: a detail of the painting* Tobias Curing His Father's Blindness *by Ignazio Hugford (Pisa 1703-Florence 1778). Commissioned by the nuns of the Benedictine convent, the work was executed around 1741 for the altar dedicated to Archangel Raphael.*

The little chapels. Inside the little chapels before the transept are tombstones dedicated to various figures linked to the grand-ducal court, testifying to the privileged relationship between the rulers and the church from the end of the 16th century on: on the left is the sepulchral monument of the auditor Giacomo Conti, an 18th-century work by Girolamo Ticciati; in the Chapel of the Virgin on the right, monuments in polychrome marble to Count Silvio Albergati, paymaster to Grand-Duke Cosimo III (17th century) and Count Francesco di Thurn, state councillor of Emperor Joseph II (end of 18th century). In the chapel on the left, on the altar of Beata Berta, there is also a wooden *Crucifix* by Andrea Ferrucci, known as Fiesole, executed for the Nero family around 1520.

Facing page, above: the little chapel before the left transept, surmounted by a curvilinear balustrade similar to the structure of the balcony of the 'coretto'. Inside are the Crucifix by Fiesole and the monument to Giacomo Conti by Girolamo Ticciati (Florence 1671-1744).
Left: the Badii-Cioli Chapel in the left transept.
In 1653 Caterina Cioli Poltri and Eleonora Badii Poli, whose coat of arms dominates the middle of the tympanum, took over the patronage of the altar dedicated to St. Jerome from the Benizzi family. A marble plate on the wall recalls the quarrel between the Frescobaldi, the direct heirs of the Benizzi, and the new patrons chosen by the nuns. The new altar, dedicated to Our Lady of the Assumption and to St. Catherine of Siena and St. Margaret of Cortona, was completed in 1654. The ciborium and the marble escutcheons (below, and facing page), a work by Florentine master craftsmen, are an original and fine example of inlay in Baroque style.

The left transept. In the Badii-Cioli altar – a typical example of a Baroque altar, with its coloured marble inlay and its graceful polygonal balustrade – is enclosed one of the most important altarpieces commissioned for the church in the 17th century, *The Assumption of the Virgin with St. Catherine of Siena and St. Margaret of Cortona*, entrusted to Volterrano by Caterina Cioli Poltri and Eleonora Badii Poli in 1677. Further along in the transept is *The Holy Trinity* (see p. 20), a recently restored painting by Carlo Portelli (Loro Ciuffenna, *ca.* 1521-Florence 1574): done for the altar with the same name, it was enlarged by Ignazio Hugford in the 18th century. Near the altar dedicated to St. Catherine, *The Marriage of the Virgin* by Gasparo Martellini (Florence 1785-1857).

The main chapel. The present arrangement shows the main chapel with the big central arch designed in the first decade of the 17th century by Ludovico Cardi, known as Cigoli, upon the commission of Piero, Francesco and Girolamo, the sons of Angelo Guicciardini. The split fronton and the surmounting coat of arms were added by Ferdinando Ruggieri during the 18th-century reconstruction.

On the vault, *The Coronation of the Virgin and Saints* painted between 1617 and 1619 by Michelangelo Cinganelli; on the side walls *The Resurrection of Christ* by Antonio Tempesta (Florence 1555-Rome 1630) and *The Crucifixion* by Lorenzo Carletti (see p. 20). The mediocre quality of these paintings makes us regret the decisions of the patron, while *The Adoration of the Shepherds* by Lorenzo Sciorina – in the centre – indirectly calls to mind the dire consequences of the bomb explosion which severely damaged the Uffizi in 1993. The work by Sciorina had originally been executed for the Florentine Church of San Giovannino dei Gesuiti; it was then transferred to Santa Felicita in 1835 to substitute the very fine *Adoration of the Shepherds* by Gherardo delle Notti, purchased by the Gallery. The

Facing page: Assumption of the Virgin with St. Catherine of Siena and St. Margaret of Cortona *by Baldassarre Franceschini, known as Volterrano (Volterra 1611-Florence 1689). The painting was completed in 1677 and placed in the Badii-Cioli Chapel. Below: the vault of the main chapel, frescoed by Michelangelo Cinganelli (Settignano, Florence ca. 1558-Florence 1635) between 1617 and 1619: in the centre,* The Coronation of the Virgin and Saints; *in the trapezoidal sections, the patron Saints of the church (St. Felicita and her Children, Benedetto, Maria Maddalena and Tobia with Archangel Raphael); inside the round 'cornices', the* Virtues. *Cinganelli's work replaced the original decoration by Neri d'Antonio (1399).*

positioning of this masterpiece in the Uffizi, intended to guarantee its maximum protection – it is known that works of art in churches are poorly lighted and not sufficiently well attended to – has unfortunately led to its destruction.

The main altar. Reconstructed in 1840 to replace the 17th-century altar by Gherardo Silvani, the main altar, like the mediocre altars in marble and stucco erected in the side chapels, testifies to the low standard reached by 19th-century interventions.

The right transept. One of the works transferred to Santa Felicita in the 19th century following the ecclesiastic suppressions was *The Meeting of St. Joachim and St. Anne*, a 16th-century painting attributed to Michele di Ridolfo del Ghirlandaio, placed on the right wall of the transept. On the back wall, now almost "unreadable", *St. John the Evangelist in Patmos* by Pisan Leonardo Cambi (1786), and an *Adoration of the Child* by Nicola Cianfanelli (1838, see p. 24).

Facing page: The Adoration of the Shepherds *by Lorenzo Sciorina. In 1835 the painting substituted a very fine work with the same subject by Gherardo delle Notti, transferred to the Uffizi and destroyed by a bomb explosion in 1993. The identification of the artist dates back to the 1988 restoration, which brought to light the date of the execution of the work (1587) and the signature of the artist. Formerly, critics had attributed the work to Santi di Tito, and later to Francesco Brina.*
Below: a detail of The Meeting of Joachim and St. Anne, *a 16th-century painting attributed to Michele Tosini known as Michele di Ridolfo del Ghirlandaio (Florence 1503-1577). Next to the meeting of the two Saints by the golden door is the representation of God the Father (above, surrounded by angels) and six Saints (below). The work, placed above the right transept, was brought to Santa Felicita in the 19th century after the ecclesiastic suppressions.*

The sacristy. Lovely example of Renaissance architecture, the sacristy has now been enriched with numerous works which once decorated the chapels. Its structure is reminiscent of the Pazzi Chapel in the cloister of Santa Croce and of the Old Sacristy in the Basilica of San Lorenzo. The ceiling is decorated in the centre by the Canigiani coat of arms and by shells in the pendentives, while the trabeation includes a relief of cherubs; sculpted in *pietra serena*, the latter, though mediocre in quality, reminds us of the lively examples by Brunelleschi in the aforementioned buildings and in the adjacent Barbadori Chapel.

The design of the sacristy, following the legacy of Giovanni Canigiani (1474), is inspired by Brunelleschi's architecture. On the right, the 'scarsella' with the Crucifix *by Pacino di Bonaguida (see p. 23) and two detached frescoes attributed to the school of Gerini. Facing page: detail of* St. Felicita and Children *by Neri di Bicci (see p. 17), on the wall facing the entrance.*

On the wall facing the entrance one can find *St. Felicita and Children*, painted by Neri di Bicci for the Nerli Chapel and recently put back in the sacristy after a long and fine restoration (see p. 16). It is a typical work by Neri, a good example of the "static", formal elegance of his paintings. Detailed documentation concerning this work can be found in the *Memoirs* of the painter, who states that he painted it for Tanai de' Nerli after 1464. The painting shows the children of the Saint in elegant 15th-century garments, their names and the order of their birth in Roman numerals. In the *predella*, scenes of their martyrdom (see p. 17).

On the wall next to the head of the transept, beside *The Adoration of the Magi* (a 15th-century Florentine work brought to Santa Felicita in 1842 after the ecclesiastic suppressions), is *The Pietà* or *Deposition from the Cross*. Commissioned by Caterina Pitti, it shows the date 1470 and has recently been attributed to the "Master of the Johnson Nativity". Transferred to the deposits of the Uffizi, it suffered severe damage during the flood of 1966; after a long restoration it was placed in the sacristy in the summer of 1999.

Facing page: Madonna and Child *by Giovanni del Biondo (Florence, active 1356-1398). The painting is mentioned among the works housed in Santa Felicita since the second half of the 18th century. Below: among the works housed in the sacristy is* The Adoration of the Magi, *attributed to Mariotto di Cristofano (first half of the 15th century). The work, already restored before the flood, underwent severe damage while it was still under restoration in the laboratories of the Superintendence of Fine Arts. The new restoration was completed in 1985 and the painting was brought back to the church at Christmas of the same year. It had been sent there in 1842 after the ecclesiastic suppressions.*

On the left wall are two frescoes depicting *The Prophets* (see p. 12). Detached in the 19th century, the fragments come from the decoration of the chapter-house, executed by artists of the school of Niccolò di Pietro Gerini.

In the *scarsella* of the sacristy, among the aforementioned *Annunciation* (see p. 13) and *Nativity* (see p. 12) by Gerini, is the large *Crucifix* by Pacino di Bonaguida, also transferred to the church in 1842 (see p. 23).

On the right wall, the lunette by Bicci di Lorenzo representing *The Mystical Marriage of St. Catherine* (1442, see p. 18) and the polyptych with *Madonna and Saints* by Taddeo Gaddi (see p. 15) surmount a glazed *terracotta* work depicting a *Madonna and Child*, recently attributed to Luca della Robbia. Among the sacred vestments and reliquaries of different styles that complete the furnishings of the sacristy, stand out the bust of St. Pulcheria, donated to the church by Sister Lucrezia Carnesecchi in 1642, and the reliquary of St. Felicita, in gilded wood in the shape of a monstrance.

Below: the sacred parament decorating the wall of the sacristy next to the transept and a detail of its twin on the opposite wall. Facing page: a fine Madonna and Child *in glazed terracotta kept in the sacristy. The work, originally in the tabernacle outside the church, on the side of Piazzetta de' Rossi, has recently been attributed to Luca della Robbia.*

The cloister. The cloister, whose arcades are now walled in, dates back to the 14th century: easily recognizable are its slender columns with their typical 'water-leaf' capitals (see p. 14). The interior side corridor houses a large fragment of mural painting from the interior of the 14th-century church. A work of the school of Gerini, the fresco represents *The Martyrdom of St. Catherine of Alexandria* (see p. 13).

The chapter-house. Of the impressive decoration by Niccolò di Pietro Gerini, executed between 1387 and 1388, have survived *The Crucifixion* on the wall facing the cloister, as well as *Christ the Saviour* and *The Seven Virtues* in the vaults. The space which houses these works is very dif-

Below: a view of the chapter-house frescoed in the 14th century by Niccolò Gerini. On the walls, Episodes from the Life of Christ *by Cosimo Ulivelli (Florence 1625-1704) and Agnolo Gori (†1678), only partially restored. On the vault are visible Christ the Saviour and the Virtues: above,* Faith, Fortitude *and* Justice. *Facing page:* The Crucifixion. *During the 1919 restoration the date of execution and the artist's signature were discovered at the bottom of the fresco.*

ferent from the original one, as the radical changes of the 17th and 18th centuries have radically reshaped a part of the *loggia* once facing the courtyard. With this work – his first commission, obtained against the tough competition of famous workshops such as those of Jacopo di Cione and Giovanni del Biondo – Gerini began a period of independent activity, specializing in mural decorations which became very fashionable (Santa Croce, Orsanmichele, Santa Verdiana and Santa Maria Primerana in Fiesole). In 1665 the 14th-century decoration, which probably covered the entire surface of the chapel, was replaced by the *Stories from the Life of Christ* by Cosimo Ulivelli and Agnolo Gori, paintings which have only partially been brought to light.

The right wall. On the altars, *St. Felicita Exhorting her Children to Martyrdom* (1810) by Giorgio Berti and *A Miracle by St. Gregory Magnus* by Francesco Vellani (1747, see p. 22). A notable exception among the 19th-century works is the painting by Antonio Ciseri representing *The Martyrdom of the Seven Maccabees* (see p. 25), destined to the chapel with the same name and positioned here in 1863. Extremely well-known (and one of the few by Ciseri with a public destination), its making is extensively documented by drawings and preliminary sketches performed in the ten years prior to the final work. The painting enjoyed great success with the public and was requested for the National Exhibition of Florence in 1861 before being placed in the church.

Right: the third chapel of the right wall, dedicated to the Most Holy Crucifix and to the Maccabees. Above the altar, The Martyrdom of the Seven Maccabees Brothers *(see p. 25), a painting by Antonio Ciseri. Facing page:* St. Felicita Exhorting her Children to Martyrdom *by Giorgio Berti (Florence 1789-1868). Executed in Rome in 1810, in 1824 the painting replaced – above the altar dedicated to St. Felicita – the work by Neri di Bicci now housed in the sacristy.*

The Barbadori-Capponi Chapel (see p. 19) is the most suggestive sight of the tour of Santa Felicita. Under the patronage of the Capponi family (from 1525 on) the 15th-century structure was covered by Pontormo's frescoes, which completely transformed the appearance of the small chapel. The stained-glass window showing The Transport of Christ to the Sepulchre by Guillaume de Marcillat is also due to the patronage of Ludovico Capponi. The work was transferred to the Capponi Palace in Via de' Bardi in the 17th century. It has now been replaced by a modern copy. Below: The Annunciation by Pontormo, on the façade wall; in the centre, the 17th-century reliquary monument to St. Carlo Borromeo, with the niche in polychrome marble by the Opificio delle Pietre Dure.

The Barbadori-Capponi Chapel ('dell'Annunziata').

The most important intervention to the church was due to the Barbadori family, previously mentioned as the patrons of the Chapel of San Frediano. This chapel, dedicated to the Virgin of the Annunciation, was commissioned to Filippo Brunelleschi by Bartolomeo Barbadori between the second and third decade of the 15th century.

While attributing to Brunelleschi "the small chapel situated in the right-hand corner of the entrance to Santa Felicita", his biographer Antonio Manetti (1480) recalled that the church "had been renewed at that time and was very beautiful". A witness to the vicissitudes of the church, and itself the object of frequent and perhaps excessive restructuring, the 15th-century outline of the chapel is nonetheless clearly visible, so that the careful observer can still distinguish the contemporary examples which had drawn the attention of Brunelleschi, such as the background of Masaccio's *Trinity* in Santa Maria Novella and the Orlandi Cardini Chapel in the Church of San Francesco in Pescia. Remnants of the original structure are the surviving capitals and the borders of the arches above the works of Pontormo, as well as the white and blue *maiolica* fragments on the floor.

For the chapel chosen as burial place of the family, Ludovico Capponi commissioned an iconographic scheme centred on the theme of the coming of Christ and the salvation of mankind. Jacopo Carucci, known as Pontormo (Pontorme, Florence 1494-Florence 1556) painted the chapel between 1525 and 1528, representing God the Father and the four Patriarchs in the vault of the cupola, the four Evangelists in the pendentives and The Annunciation on the right wall (on the left and on the following pages, details of The Angel of the Annunciation and The Virgin). The frescoes on the vault described by Giorgio Vasari were unfortunately destroyed between 1765 and 1767, when the grand-ducal family had the domes of the two side chapels lowered to enlarge the 'coretto'.

The depiction of the Evangelists in the pendentives of the vault evokes the theme of the Good News leading to salvation. Of the four 'tondi', only the one representing St. John (below) is unanimously attributed to Pontormo.

Between 1525 and 1528 the pictorial decoration by Pontormo – a new and vital architectural event inside the old church – "overlapped" Brunelleschi's architectural structure.

Through this intervention – commissioned by Ludovico Capponi, then patron of the chapel – the structure lost its Renaissance features to take on a truly dynamic Mannerist style. The explosion of freedom expressed in the interior before the destructive interventions of the 17th and 18th centuries did justice to Pontormo's art, to his constant restlessness and to "the extravagant eccentricity of his mind". As Vasari says, Pontormo "was never contented with anything".

The original 15th- and 16th-century character of the chapel was revived by the restoration of the Superintendence of Fine Arts in 1936. This restoration was aimed at retrieving the original complex which had been profoundly altered – in its structural elements, decorations and colours – by the numerous interventions and changes effected from the 16th century on. The decorations brought to light are extremely forceful, especially when imagined in the original version, which extensively employed the gold and blue of the Barbadori insignia. With their rich and bright colours, now irretrievably lost, these decorative elements no doubt established a very strong bond with Pontormo's work. This covered the entire surface of the interi-

One of the assistants of Pontormo in Santa Felicita was Agnolo di Cosimo Tori known as Bronzino (Florence 1503-1572), who painted the 'tondo' representing St. Matthew the Evangelist. *The original painting, still to be restored, has been replaced by a copy.*

Above, from left to right:
St. Mark and St. Luke *conclude the cycle of 'tondi' representing the Evangelists. Some critics have recognized in these paintings the hand of Bronzino. Right: the celebrated* Deposition from the Cross, *above the altar of the chapel. Pontormo, who had been a pupil of Piero di Cosimo, Leonardo da Vinci and Andrea del Sarto, began his activity in Santa Felicita after having frescoed the Medici Villa of Poggio a Caiano and the Certosa of Galluzzo. According to Vasari, the artist, fully aware of the innovative impact of his work, prevented all access to the chapel by barring the entrance with high panels – which Vasari calls "turate" – for the entire duration of the work.*

or, transforming it completely. In the vault of the *cupola* were frescoed *God the Father and the Four Patriarchs* (fresco destroyed in 1767); in the *tondi, The Four Evangelists* (among whom the *St. Matthew* by his pupil Agnolo Bronzino), and on the right wall the graceful figures of *The Angel of the Annunciation* and of *The Virgin*, illuminated by the light filtering through the window. A copy of *The Transport of Christ to the Sepulchre* by Guillaume de Marcillat can now be seen on the small window, while between the angel and the Virgin is the reliquary monument of St. Carlo Borromeo, an elegant work executed in the 17th century by the Opificio delle Pietre Dure ('Workshop of Semi-Precious Stone'). It was probably based on a drawing sent from Rome together with the portrait and relics of the Saint.

Lastly, on the wall above the altar is a painting with *The Deposition* or *Pietà*, in accordance with the new dedication of the chapel ordered by Ludovico Capponi: an extraordinary, unreal mass of entwined bodies moving to an imaginary rhythm. This masterpiece is the finest work of the artist, who reaches here a peak of concentrated spirituality and dramatic intensity. The decoration as a whole – a true pictorial and emotional turmoil – breathed new life into Brunelleschi's balanced and rigorous architecture.

The church is a unusual visiting place for tourists and hasty visitors; still, Pontormo's ecstatic masterpieces have drawn the attention of admirers and famous scholars, such as Niccolò Tommaseo and Filippo De Pisis. According to critics, in this work "form... transcends the contents to

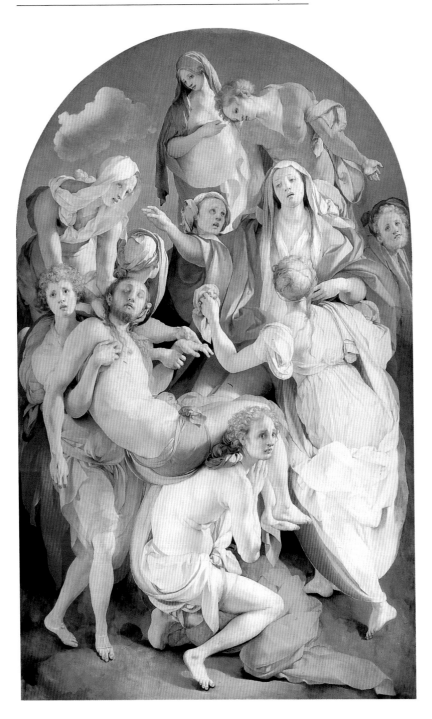

The Deposition, *which is considered Pontormo's masterpiece, was conceived as the true climax of the themes which form the iconographic plan of the chapel. A suspended feeling of exhaustion and expectation marks the final moment of separation from earthly life. Right: the two youths bearing the body of Christ (already devoid of the evident signs of martyrdom) raise the Son towards God the Father, formerly depicted in the vault. As Giorgio Vasari critically observed, this complex composition by Pontormo revolutionized the classical canons of proportion, deforming the limbs of the figures and placing them in an unreal perspective. Hence, Mary emerges near the top of the inextricable mass of bodies represented in the painting (on the facing page, below, a detail), to the point of towering above the female figure moving towards her. Facing page, above: a detail of the figure behind the Virgin which critics believe to be a self-portrait of Pontormo.*

express, above all, itself – an already modern concept of 'art for art's sake' (*art pour l'art*)" (L. Berti); "just as altogether new and subtle are the tones of the colours, pale and fresh like shades of squashed grass and juices of spring flowers" (L. Briganti). Now that we know the 'real' colours of the *Tondo Doni* and of the recently restored Sistine Chapel, we can fully appreciate the dependence of Pontormo and numerous Mannerists on Michelangelo, with regard not only to formal premises, but also and above all to his choice of colours.

Bibliography

Besides numerous documents and manuscripts existing in the archives of the rectory of Santa Felicita and the State Archives of Florence one may consult:

F. BOCCHI-G. CINELLI, *Le Bellezze della città di Firenze*, Florence 1677.

G. RICHA, *Notizie Istoriche delle Chiese Fiorentine divise ne' suoi quartieri*, IX, Florence 1761.

G. BALOCCHI, *Illustrazione dell'I. e R. Chiesa Parrocchiale di S. Felicita che può servire di guida all'osservatore*, Florence 1828.

A. COCCHI, *Le chiese di Firenze dal sec. IV al sec. XX*, Florence 1903.

P. FONTANA, *Die Cappella Barbadori in Santa Felicita in Florenz*, "Mitteilungen des Kunsthistorischen Instituts in Florenz", 1931-1932.

P. SANPAOLESI, *La Chiesa di S. Felicita in Firenze*, "Rivista d'Arte", 2a s., 6, 1934.

R. NICCOLI, *Su alcuni recenti saggi eseguiti alla brunelleschiana cappella Barbadori in Santa Felicita*, in Atti del I Congresso Nazionale di Storia dell'Architettura (1936), Florence 1938.

W. PAATZ-E. PAATZ, *Die Kirchen von Florenz*, II, Frankfurt a/M. 1941.

J. COX, *Pontormo's drawings from the destroyed vault of the Capponi chapel*, "The Burlington Magazine", 634, 1956.

G. MAETZKE, *Firenze. Resti di basilica cimiteriale sotto Santa Felicita*, "Atti dell'Accademia Nazionale dei Lincei. Notizie degli scavi di Antichità", 12, 7, 1957.

U. SCHLEGEL, *La cappella Barbadori e l'architettura fiorentina del primo Rinascimento*, "Rivista d'Arte", 3a s., 1957 [1959].

H. SAALMAN, *Filippo Brunelleschi: capital studies*, "The Art Bulletin", 40, 2, 1958.

H. SAALMAN, *Further notes on the cappella Barbadori in S. Felicita*, "The Burlington Magazine", 665, 1958.

L. BERTI, *Pontormo*, Florence 1964.

K.W. FORSTER, *Pontormo*, Munich 1966.

L. MOSIICI, *Le carte del Monastero di S. Felicita di Firenze*, Florence 1969.

A. BUSIGNANI-R. BENCINI, *Le chiese di Firenze. Quartiere di S. Spirito*, Florence 1974.

M. MOSCO, *Itinerario di Firenze barocca*, Florence 1974.

P. DEGL'INNOCENTI, *Conformazione e storia della Piazza di S. Felicita*, "Studi e Documenti di Architettura", 7, 1978.

F. FIORELLI MALESCI, *La chiesa di Santa Felicita a Firenze*, Firenze 1986.

G. CORTI, *Il "Registro de' mandati" dell'ambasciatore granducale Pietro Guicciardini e la committenza artistica fiorentina a Roma nel secondo decennio del Seicento*, "Paragone", 473, 1989.

G. PAPI, *Novità sul soggiorno italiano di G. Honthorst*, "Paragone", 479-481, 1990.

Index

Printed in Italy by Alpilito - Florence
February 2000